Clermont

Clermont

Bruce E. Naramore
and Reed Sparling

With a foreword by
J. Winthrop Aldrich

Photographs by
Chris Kendall and
Tracie Rozhon

PUBLISHED BY THE FRIENDS OF CLERMONT

A project of the Friends of Clermont, and its generous members and supporters.

Additional funding provided by a grant from Furthermore: a program of the J. M. Kaplan Fund.

Concept and Art Direction: Tracie Rozhon
Design and Composition: John Bernstein Design, Inc.
Printed in China by Oceanic Graphic Printing (USA), Inc.

The Friends of Clermont, chartered by the New York State Department of Education in 1977, is a not-for-profit organization formed to support and supplement museum education and historic preservation programs at Clermont State Historic Site. Clermont, a United States National Historic Landmark, is administered by the New York State Office of Parks, Recreation, and Historic Preservation, Taconic Region.

Friends of Clermont
87 Clermont Avenue, Germantown, NY 12526
(518) 537-6622 · www.friendsofclermont.org

ISBN: 978-0-578-05250-2

Contents

7   Foreword   by J. Winthrop Aldrich

10   Clermont's Past: The Livingstons and
Their Riverfront House   by Reed Sparling

23   Portfolio: The Estate through the Seasons

        The Gardens
        The Cottages
        The Barns
        The Ruins

38   Interiors: A Guide to the Rooms
by Bruce E. Naramore

        Center Hall and Main Stairs
        Drawing Room
        The Study
        The Library
        Dining Room
        The Kitchen and Pantry
        Upstairs Hall
        Alice Livingston's Bedroom
        The Blue Guest Bedroom
        Bathrooms
        Servants' Rooms

84   Festivities

88   Chronology

        Owners and Heads-of-Household
        Timeline

Foreword

*W*elcome to Clermont! You are in good company: George Washington and his wife preceded you here in 1782 (Martha stayed in a basement room to be cool during a steamy June visit) and a festive ball was held on September 16, 1824, in honor of the visit of the elderly Marquis de Lafayette, whose young French equerries misjudged the potency of Columbia County applejack and crashed through a glass door (they were forgiven—it was a French door).

And then there was Robert Fulton, who on August 18, 1807, made landfall at the dock here aboard the steamboat that he and Chancellor Livingston had developed. His arrival followed 24 hours of uninterrupted steam navigation from lower Manhattan—an epochal voyage of invention. Several months later Fulton entered into a second Livingston partnership when he married the Chancellor's kinswoman Harriet Livingston.

Another memorable moment in the presence of company here is described in a gossipy letter relating the death from a stroke of the indomitable matriarch Margaret Beekman Livingston, aged 76:

> July 14, 1800....The old Lady of Clermont took her leave of this world with great éclat. She walked about the gardens and did business all the morning and had several of her friends to dinner, of which she amply partook. In taking a glass of wine she found her right hand failing, changed it to her left, soon fell in a fit and expired without a groan.

It should be no surprise that many strong, independent-minded women sprouted from these Livingston roots, among them Elizabeth Cady Stanton and Eleanor Roosevelt.

The most renowned Livingston to bear that surname was Chancellor Robert R. Livingston, a dean of the American Enlightenment for whom patronage of the arts and sciences was a passion. (His grandson, Montgomery Livingston, who lived here, was an accomplished landscape painter in the Hudson River School.) The Chancellor also manifested his family's hereditary inclination toward public service, which—albeit less grandly—carried down to his son-in-law, Edward P. Livingston of Clermont, who was elected Lieutenant Governor of New York in 1830, and to his great-grandson John Henry Livingston, who in 1898 narrowly missed being elected to Congress as a Democrat in this strongly Republican district.

Polish patriot Julian Niemcewicz, who visited in 1798, wrote:

> Because they marry among themselves, their estates are increased rather than broken up. The mother of the Chancellor, heiress to the rich Beekman family, brought more than one hundred thousand acres of land to the Livingston estate.... The most attractive conversation for these lovers of republican equality is about the ancient lineage of their family, about the arms of the Livingstons, about the ramifications of the family and the extent of their relationships, etc....One of the greatest advantages of living here on this beautiful river is the pleasant neighbors who are in good accord. The trunk of the Livingston family is wide; it spreads its branches in all directions. All these people are well-to-do, polite, related, closely-knit in friendships and sentiment.

Today the Clermont historic site encompasses 500 acres, down from 13,000 two centuries ago. In the 1840s Andrew Jackson Downing observed that Clermont was "the showplace of the last age," noting that in the layout and practical uses of the grounds it was very much an eighteenth-century property—something succeeding generations showed little interest in changing. In 1889 Charles Eliot, pioneering conservationist and a partner in the Olmsted landscape architecture firm, wrote that although Clermont's owners were often compelled to be away on business or public duties, "they always returned to Clermont as to their one permanent home—so strong...was their old English liking for country life and country leisure."

Katharine Livingston and Lawrence Timpson posed with their wedding party under a large black walnut tree at Clermont in 1900. Members of the wedding party arrived from New York City and Philadelphia by private railroad car.

Recognition of the significance of Clermont's associations and the national importance of its architecture, landscape, and collections continues unabated. The house was documented in volume 2 of *Great Georgian Houses of America* (1937), commissioned by the privately funded Architects' Emergency Committee during the Depression. Following acquisition by the State of New York in 1962, the entire property was listed on the National Register of Historic Places (1971), designated a National Historic Landmark (1972), and identified as a key element in both the Hudson River National Historic Landmark District (1990) and in the Hudson River Valley National Heritage Area (1996). For more than thirty years the nonprofit, member-supported Friends of Clermont has effectively collaborated with the State in protecting, enhancing, and promoting this special place. The handsome book you are holding is another product of this endeavor.

The Livingstons would have approved. Now Clermont belongs to the people. Cherish the legacy.

— J. Winthrop Aldrich
New York State Deputy Commissioner for Historic Preservation

Clermont's Past: The Livingstons and Their Riverfront House

by Reed Sparling

The fanlighted doorway of Clermont affords one of the Hudson Valley's most spectacular views, stretching across the Hudson River to the Catskill Mountains. The house itself is equally remarkable, home to seven generations of Livingstons who defined and cherished our nation's past. They settled portions of the American wilderness, took part in the colonists' revolt, and, for those staying at Clermont, paid dearly when their home was torched by the British. They played significant roles in establishing our democracy and expanding its boundaries. Their partnership with Robert Fulton in creating the first successful steamboat revolutionized transportation and commerce. By tenaciously preserving Clermont and its magnificent grounds, they have ensured that these stories would continue to be told.

Clermont was constructed between 1740 and 1750 by Robert Livingston Jr. (1688–1775). It was situated on land acquired in 1686 by his father, Robert Livingston Sr. (1654–1728), by authority of King James II, just a dozen years after Dutch

New Netherland finally became British New York. In 1663, Robert Sr.'s father, a nonconformist minister, had been ejected from Scotland on religious grounds and his son, then only eight, went with him to Rotterdam. He was soon fluent in Dutch and began to learn about mercantile life.

When his father died in 1672, Robert Sr. returned briefly to Scotland with his mother but soon decided to immigrate to America, settling in Albany in 1674. There the ambitious 20-year-old quickly made himself indispensable to the Dutch, the English, and the Iroquois, gaining a foothold in the lucrative fur trade. His 1679 marriage to the young widow of the province's leading landowner all but guaranteed his success.

Abraham Delanoy's portrait of Philip Livingston is displayed in Clermont's drawing room. Philip signed the Declaration of Independence for New York, while his cousin, the Chancellor (who had helped write it) was away on business in the Hudson Valley.

The royal patent secured by Robert granted him the privileges of a manor lord and 160,000 wilderness acres, stretching ten miles along the Hudson River's east bank and eastward to the border of present-day Massachusetts. Over the next 150 years, these lands would be cleared and cultivated by tenant farmers working under a leasehold system dating back to the Middle Ages.

In addition to paying rent, the tenants were required to perform several days of work per year for their landlord. Usually these leaseholds were durable, lasting for three generations, thereby justifying the work in clearing the land, building structures, and establishing the farmstead.

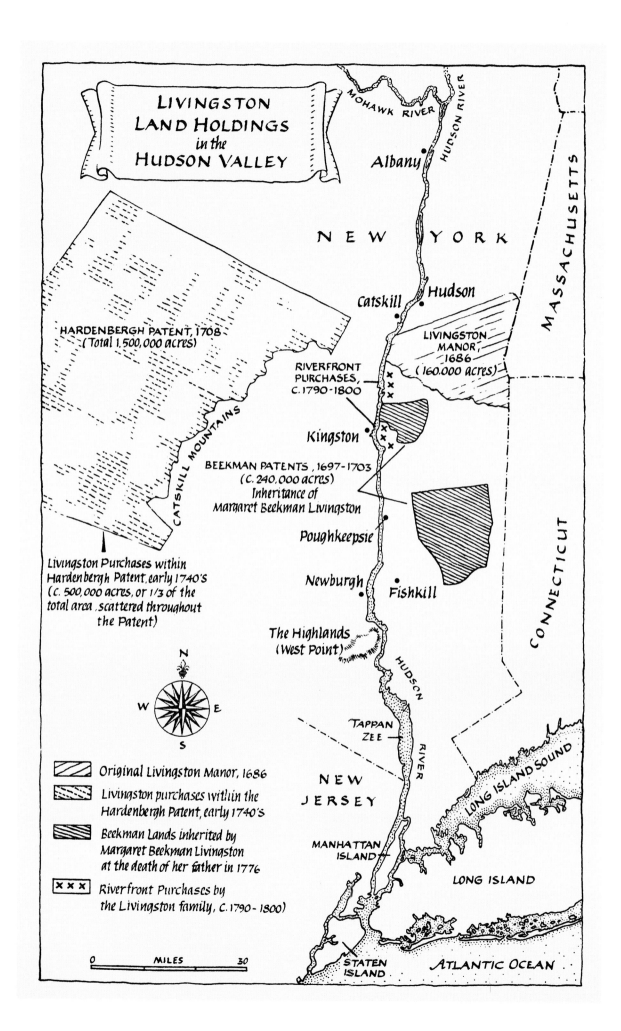

LIVINGSTON
LAND HOLDINGS
in the
HUDSON VALLEY

MOHAWK RIVER

HUDSON RIVER

Albany

N E W   Y O R K

MASSACHUSETTS

Catskill •Hudson

LIVINGSTON
MANOR,
1686
(160,000 acres)

HARDENBERGH PATENT, 1708
(Total 1,500,000 acres)

RIVERFRONT
PURCHASES,
C.1790-1800

CATSKILL MOUNTAINS

Kingston

BEEKMAN PATENTS, 1697-1703
(C. 240,000 acres)
Inheritance of
Margaret Beekman Livingston

Poughkeepsie

CONNECTICUT

Livingston Purchases within
Hardenbergh Patent, early 1740's
(c. 500,000 acres, or 1/3 of the
total area, scattered throughout
the Patent)

Newburgh • Fishkill

The Highlands
(West Point)

HUDSON

N
W   E
S

TAPPAN
ZEE

RIVER

LONG ISLAND SOUND

N E W
J E R S E Y

MANHATTAN
ISLAND

LONG ISLAND

Original Livingston Manor, 1686

Livingston purchases within the
Hardenbergh Patent, early 1740's

Beekman Lands inherited by
Margaret Beekman Livingston
at the death of her father in 1776

X X X   Riverfront Purchases by
the Livingston family, c. 1790-1800

STATEN
ISLAND

ATLANTIC OCEAN

0   MILES   30

According to family legend, skullduggery led to Clermont's existence. As the third son, Robert Jr. had no expectations of an inheritance: British law required all of Livingston Manor to pass to his eldest brother upon their father's death. However, one day young Robert noticed several Indians lurking near the manor house, erected at the mouth of the Roeliff Jansen Kill—a twist on this tale identifies the malefactors as rebellious slaves! As he lay in bed that night, he was startled by a rustling in the chimney and saw a pair of legs emerge from the flue. Leaping up, Robert seized the trespasser and made him confess to a plot to murder and rob the family. As a reward for saving their lives, Robert's father bequeathed him a 13,000-acre tract at the southwest corner of his estate.

An indifferent lawyer and a committed bon vivant whose needs often exceeded his means, Robert Jr. became a man reborn after inheriting the land in 1728. Now, at age forty, he had a purpose. He turned out to be a smart businessman in a long line of astute Livingston merchants. With hefty profits secured from privateering and provisioning British troops (and a sizable inheritance), he soon bought even more property—500,000 acres in the Catskills.

Robert constructed a Georgian-style mansion, befitting his status as a country squire, on a bluff above the river. Originally, he called it *Claremont,* or *Claremount*—it is spelled both ways in his letters.

After the Revolutionary War, the Livingstons, in keeping with the widespread love of all things French, spelled it *Clermont,* or "clear mountain." It's hard to imagine a more fitting name.

A nineteenth-century visitor described how the Catskills furnish an "elegant display of light and shade occasioned by their irregularity, their fine blue color, the climbing of the mists up their sides, the intervention of the clouds which cap their summits or shroud their sides only, with their occasional reflections from the surface of the Hudson." Such a vista, the writer proclaimed, was "no where exceeded in this country."

In his new home, "Robert of Clermont" (also known as "Robert the Builder") devoted himself to scholarly pursuits and confined his extravagance to spoiling his grandchildren, a far cry from his self-indulgent past. One thing, however, remained constant—his attire. Despite rapidly changing fashions in the eighteenth century, Robert stuck to his sartorial guns, opting for powdered wigs, knee-length breeches, and square-toed shoes. "These were retained in his service not to effect a singularity, but because he thought it ridiculous, at his time of life, to allow the quick succession of fashion," explained his grandson Edward.

The Judge and His Formidable Wife

Robert's sole heir, his son Robert (1718–1775), possessed ambition in spades. A brilliant lawyer, he rose in the political ranks to serve on the Provincial Assembly, the Supreme Court, and the Admiralty Court. In an age when nepotism usually determined how far a man could go, the success of "Robert the Judge" was primarily the result of his acumen combined with a personality so engaging it prompted one political rival to admit, "I do not believe you have an enemy in the world."

It didn't hurt that he had a dream wife. The only surviving child of a prominent Dutchess County landowner, Margaret Beekman (1724–1800) stood to inherit 100,000 acres, but she brought much more than property to her 1742 marriage. Chief among her assets, according to one biographer, was "an endowment of exceptional character, good common-sense and rare executive capacity."

All came in handy when Robert, frequently absent while tending to political and business affairs, left Margaret in charge of the home front, including the couple's ten children. Robert's correspondence with Margaret attests that this was a love match: "You are the cordial drop with which Heaven has graciously thought fit to sweeten my cup," he exclaimed in one letter.

Margaret Livingston's mettle was put to the test during the American Revolution. It fell upon her to oversee the family's cumbersome move from Manhattan to Clermont, where they planned to sit out the conflict. Shortly after the Battle of Bunker Hill in 1775, she lost her father-in-law. Six

Margaret Beekman Livingston, the Grande Dame of the Hudson Valley, in a 1794 portrait by Gilbert Stuart.

months later, her husband and her father died within days of each other. While mourning for them, news was received that the husband of her daughter Janet, General Richard Montgomery, had been killed leading the failed American assault on Quebec.

Title to Clermont passed to Margaret's son Robert, but he was busy helping to unite the rebellious thirteen colonies. As a member of the Second Continental Congress, he worked with Thomas Jefferson, John Adams, Roger Sherman, and Benjamin Franklin to draft the Declaration of Independence. Running the family estate rested on Margaret's shoulders, and she proved more than equal to the task.

In October 1777 the war arrived on Clermont's doorstep via a British armada sailing upriver from New York City to provide support for General John Burgoyne's army, whose march from Canada was foundering north of Albany. The force already had stormed two forts in the Hudson Highlands and burned Kingston, the first capital of the new New York State. The next inviting target was the riverfront seat of the rebel Livingstons.

Learning of the imminent danger, Margaret Livingston took action—after first declining an offer of protection from a wounded British officer recuperating at Clermont. (She stead-fastly refused to seek aid from an enemy of her country.) She directed that the family's possessions be loaded onto all available carts and wagons; silver and other valuables were buried in the surrounding woods.

The family, heading for safety in Connecticut, was barely a mile from the house when their backward glances detected smoke billowing above Clermont. Only its brick walls survived the blaze; the home Margaret's son Robert had erected nearby was destroyed as well.

Within a year Margaret was superintending Clermont's reconstruction on its original foundation. She petitioned an old family friend and the state's new governor, George Clinton, to release estate workers from their militia duties so they could complete the work— this while the redcoats were still menacing the mid-Hudson Valley! Clinton complied.

Prominent marine artist Samuel Ward Stanton took some artistic license in his 1909 painting of "The Dock at Clermont" by placing the wharf to the north, rather than to the south, of the house.

Whether he knew it or not, the governor owed Margaret Livingston a huge debt. When her son Robert, John Jay, and other state leaders had hit a roadblock in their search for a suitable gubernatorial candidate, it is said that she had suggested Clinton. It was a wise choice: he held the post for the next twenty-one years, leaving it only to accept the vice-presidency.

The current layout of Clermont's center hall and four flanking rooms reflects the postwar rebuilding. Here Margaret Livingston resumed a life dedicated to educating her children and grandchildren, and being a welcoming hostess.

Maintaining her legendary hospitality was an arduous task. According to a contemporary account, "There were great preparations in the kitchen against winter. Then all hands were busy, pickling beef and pork, curing hams, preparing sausages. The good housewife had always well filled shelves of mince-meat, cheese and preserves, apples were plenty and the buckwheat cake regularly appeared at breakfast. As soon as the river was free from ice, the shad made their appearance, then calves and lambs were due, and wild ducks and geese flew northwards, so by spring there would be nothing to complain of in the way of fare." Margaret was especially protective of her china; it is said she refused to let her servants clean it, preferring to wash and dry every piece herself.

The Chancellor and Mr. Fulton

By far Clermont's most illustrious resident was Margaret's son Robert (1746−1813), known as "the Chancellor" because of a state judicial position he held in which, among other tasks, he administered the first oath of office to President George Washington on the balcony of Manhattan's Federal Hall in 1789.

A law partner of John Jay, he served as Secretary of Foreign Affairs—comparable to today's Secretary of State—under the Articles of Confederation. He played a leading role in New York's adoption of the U.S. Constitution. As President Jefferson's Minister to France, he is usually credited with initiating and negotiating the 1803 Louisiana Purchase, which doubled the size of the country. The Chancellor was a man of vision. Learning while in France of experiments conducted by Robert Fulton to perfect the steamboat, he bankrolled the inventor, helped to develop the vessel, and secured a monopoly for their ships on the Hudson River. On the first upriver voyage from New York City in 1807 Fulton stopped at Clermont to pay his respects. The success of the craft, dubbed by wags a "tea kettle on a raft," revolutionized transportation on the Hudson and waterways across America. (Years later the ship became popularly known as the *Clermont*.)

Chancellor Robert R. Livingston, left, (1746–1813), painted by Gilbert Stuart in 1794. One of four originals made for the family, this portrait has hung in Clermont for generations.

Benjamin West's oil portrait of Robert Fulton (1765–1815) was executed in 1806, a year before his epochal steamboat voyage up the Hudson.

Successive generations at Clermont continued to cherish the house, its furnishings, and the grounds, although the acreage was drastically reduced following the abolishment of long-term leaseholds in 1846. Nevertheless, from the lands inherited from her father, Margaret Livingston, herself a canny businesswoman, provided sizable properties for each of her children.

The story of that inheritance is fascinating, a rare, early example of women's independence. In those days, a woman's property belonged to her husband outright; the only way she could hold it personally was as a widow or spinster. Because Margaret's husband died before her father, she was entitled to her father's estate. The Chancellor already had inherited what is today the entire Town of Clermont (including, of course, the Clermont estate) and a half million acres in the Catskills. Margaret divided her lands, located in Dutchess and Ulster counties, among her nine younger children, the allotment being made by the drawing of straws. Nevertheless, the drawing favored her sons, by giving them about one-third more land, presumably because they would have wives and children to support.

Samuel Ward Stanton imagined the first steamboat about to land at the Clermont dock in this 1908 pencil sketch.

Eventually, so many of Margaret Livingston's children built homes along the Hudson that at one point it was suggested the region be renamed "Livingston Valley." Unfortunately, in 1909 the Chancellor's second house, built after the Revolution, was destroyed by fire. Its ruins overlook the river just south of Clermont's main parking area, near several hiking trails.

The Next Generation

Over the decades, the family seat underwent numerous "improvements." Two wings—one for the kitchen, the other for bedrooms—were added in 1814 and 1831, respectively. In 1851 the railroad intruded at the foot of the bluff, and in 1874 the mansion was topped by a new third floor under a mansard roof. In 1893 a second and third floor were added to the south wing; the main floor of the wing was remodeled as a billiard room. Elsewhere in the house, a new kitchen and indoor plumbing were installed. Finally, a Colonial Revival restyling was completed in the 1920s. The fragrant Lilac Walk was added in 1820; the formal garden was created in the early twentieth century.

Honoria and Janet Livingston, aged 7 and 5, at the nursery window (1915).

A modest farm continued to support the needs of the family and their employees, and eventually automobiles supplanted horses. The historic riverfront pier, still evident at the time of the Hudson-Fulton celebration in 1909, started slipping away.

John Henry Livingston, a great-grandson of Chancellor Livingston and Clermont's owner in the early twentieth century, died in 1927. Thereafter, his widow, Alice Delafield Clarkson Livingston, and their two daughters, Honoria and Janet, stayed on at Clermont, drastically economizing during the Depression and World War II. Alice kept up her activities as a gardener, photographer, and sculptor, while Janet, who never married, became a banker and weekend aviator. In 1931 Honoria married an Irishman, Reginald McVitty, in the last family wedding held at Clermont during the family's owner-ship. The couple took up residence in Sylvan Cottage, just inside the front gate. Alice and Janet spent their last years in the former Gardener's Cottage.

Determined that the estate and its treasures would remain intact for all to enjoy, in 1962 the family sold Clermont and most of its surrounding land to the State of New York, simultaneously donating the mansion's furnishings. Subsequently, the remainder of the property and a modest endowment were donated by Honoria McVitty (1909–2000). She and her sister were devoted conservationists, reflecting a passionate love of the land that had become imprinted in Livingston genes across the generations. It is a pervasive ethos that all are now invited to share, and nowhere is it more affecting than at this historically compelling and deeply evocative estate. ✳

Sisters Janet Livingston (above) and Honoria McVitty (below) were the last members of the Livingston family to live at Clermont. These photographs were taken on the grounds of Sylvan Cottage in the 1960s.

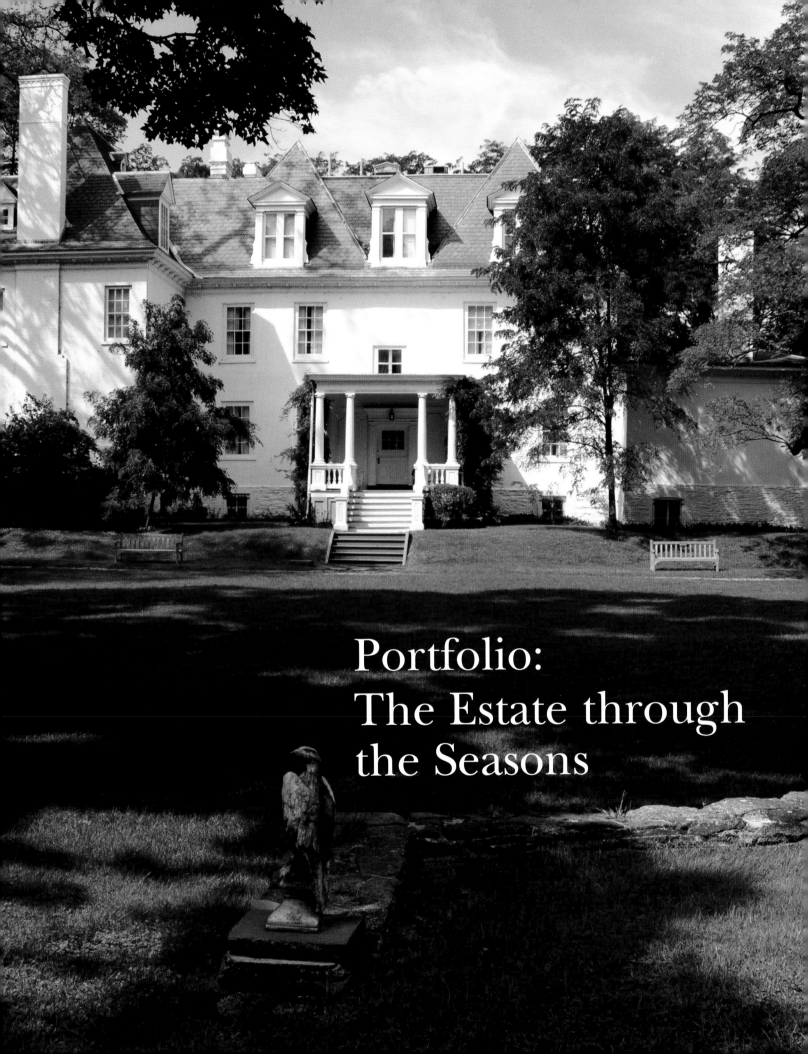

Portfolio:
The Estate through
the Seasons

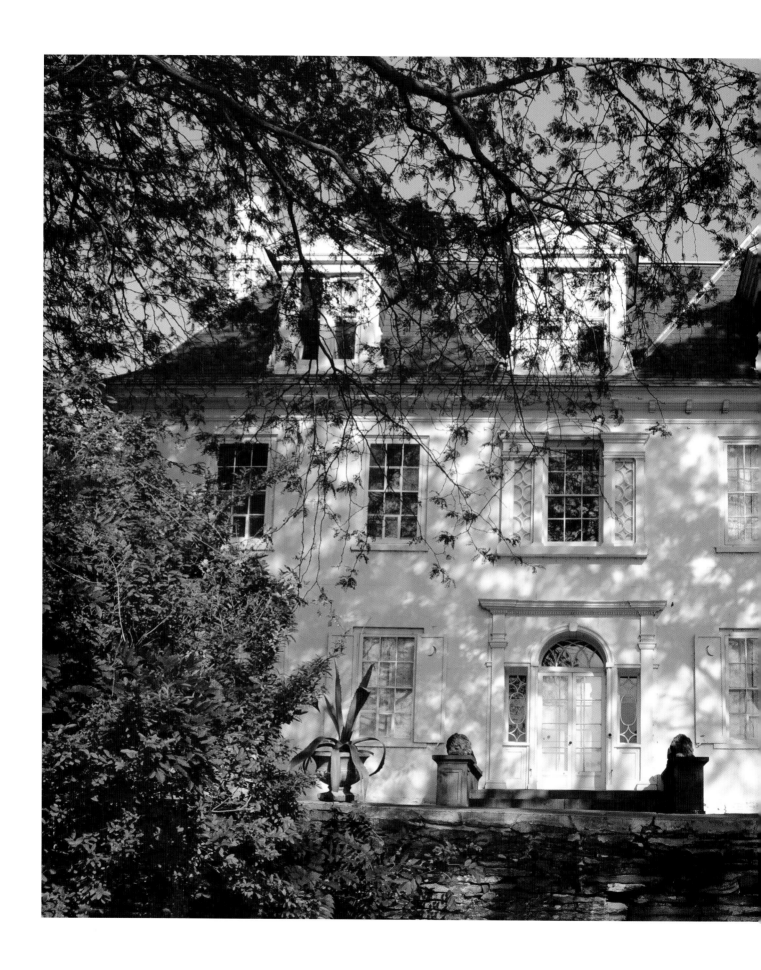

The Gardens

Elements of Clermont's eighteenth century landscape can still be viewed by the discerning visitor. The terrace on the east side of the mansion and many of the towering black locusts on the estate would have been familiar sights to Margaret Beekman Livingston and her family. The Lilac Walk, which comes to life magnificently every May, was planted in the early nineteenth century by Edward P. Livingston. When one thinks of the gardens of Clermont today, however, the several formal gardens created by Alice Livingston between 1908 and 1940 most readily come to mind. Mrs. Livingston took inspiration from her travels and the writings of horticulturalists such as Gertrude Jeykll to create her walled Italian garden and "Wilderness" garden. The cutting garden and rose garden provided fragrance and natural beauty to the interior of the mansion between May and September.

The bust of the woman in the Walled Garden was acquired by Alice Livingston at auction in the 1950s. It had previously ornamented the gardens at the Wyatt estate in Barrytown.

Clermont Cottage, or
The Gardener's Cottage

The Gardener's Cottage was built between 1790 and 1800 for Chancellor Livingston's farm manager, and, until the Second World War, housed the families of a succession of farm workers, gardeners and domestic staff. After the Japanese attack on Pearl Harbor, with fuel becoming scarce, Alice Livingston closed up "the big house" and moved into this cottage. In 1944 Mrs. Livingston expanded, adding a garage with an apartment above for her unmarried daughter Janet. After the defeat of the Axis powers, Mrs. Livingston tried to move back to the main house but found the ancient plumbing, suspect heating and the sheer size of the house unmanageable, and decided to stay there, opening the big house only during the summer and for special occasions. In 1953, she enlarged the house again, adding a modern kitchen, dining room and guest bedroom. The cottage is presently being restored by the Friends of Clermont for use as a research library and meeting rooms.

Sylvan Cottage

According to one family story, this cottage was built by Margaret Beekman Livingston as a temporary residence from which she oversaw the rebuilding of her Georgian mansion after it was burned by the British in 1777. Whenever it was built, the little house served off and on as Clermont's gatekeeper's cottage, but often hosted honeymooning couples in the Livingston family while their much grander homes along the Hudson were being built— hence, it has also been called "The Honeymoon Cottage." Following Honoria Livingston's marriage to Reginald "Rex" McVitty in 1931, the couple followed tradition by moving into Sylvan Cottage, and Mr. McVitty kept an amusing diary of his time there and in Florida, where they spent the warmer months. After their deaths—he in 1979, she in 2000—the property was left to the State of New York.

The Cow Barn

Although most of Clermont's outbuildings have long since fallen in upon their foundations, the red barn across "The Avenue" from Clermont Cottage stands as a reminder that Clermont was for most of its history a working farm. During the early years of the Republic, Chancellor Robert R. Livingston's farm was known throughout the country for his experiments with fertilizers, imported fruits and vegetables and Merino sheep. Later generations focused on developing the estate's apple orchards. The red barn was built following the Civil War by John Henry Livingston, who established a commercial dairy at Clermont in the 1880s. During the twentieth century the barn housed the Livingston family's milk cows and Janet Livingston's horse, "Captain Kidd."

The Carriage Barn

This distinctive green barn is the first building visitors see when they arrive at Clermont. The carriage barn was used to stable horses and was home to the Livingston's carriages and sleighs before they bought their first automobile in 1919. John Henry Livingston also stored his "ice yacht," the Arrow, there. Restored in the 1980's, the building now contains the historic site's orientation exhibits and a museum shop.

The Ruins

The ruins south of Clermont's main parking lot were once one of the grandest private homes in the United States. Chancellor Robert R. Livingston built the French neo-classical mansion he called "Clermont" in the 1790s as his country seat. It was later called "New Clermont" to distinguish it from the older Georgian mansion that was the home of the Chancellor's mother. "New Clermont" was sold to the Clarkson sisters at auction after Montgomery Livingston's death in 1855 and was rechristened "Idele." The home was reacquired by John Henry Livingston in the early twentieth century and was renamed "Arryl House" (the phonetic rendering of the Chancellor's initials: RRL). The house was destroyed in a grass fire of undetermined origin on a windy November evening in 1909. Rather than rebuild, the Livingstons decided to allow nature to take its course and the ruins were retained as a picturesque reminder of Clermont's past glory.

37

Interiors:
A Guide to the Rooms

by Bruce E. Naramore

Center Hall and Main Stairs

During most of Clermont's long history visitors would arrive at the west stairway to the house and enter through the wide "Dutch" door. As they entered the center hall they would immediately note that this was the home of an important family with long-established roots in the Hudson Valley. To either side of the hall are portraits of the three Lords of Livingston Manor, made from the originals hanging in other family homes. John Henry Livingston commissioned Charles Lang to make these copies in 1909, at the time of the Hudson-Fulton Celebration.

Further down the hall was a portrait of Clermont's most distinguished resident, Chancellor Robert R. Livingston. This portrait, along with a companion image of the Chancellor's mother, Margaret Beekman Livingston, was painted by Gilbert Stuart in 1794.

Next to the portrait of the Chancellor is a tall case clock, still in working condition. The works, made in London by Daniel Wood circa 1735, are believed to have been saved from the fire that destroyed the house in 1777. The case, probably crafted in New York City after the Revolution, replaced the case burned by the British.

The portrait above the marble-topped pier table depicts Philip Livingston, second Lord of Livingston Manor and father of a signer of the Declaration of Independence, also named Philip Livingston.

Family tradition surrounding the clock relates a prank played by the Livingston children when the Rev. John Christopher Hartwick (for whom Hartwick College at Oneonta, N.Y. is named) visited the home in 1796. Rev. Hartwick was feeling ill and told the family of a premonition that he would die that night at the stroke of midnight. Hoping to sooth their anxious guest, the children secretly moved the hands of the clock forward one hour. When the clock chimed twelve the children pointed out to Rev. Hartwick that he was still alive and could sleep peacefully. But at the stroke of one, which was actually midnight, he collapsed. It is true that Rev. Hartwick died at Clermont in 1796, but whether he spent his last night at Margaret Livingston's house or at the adjoining home of her son, the Chancellor, is not known.

The Livingston family accessed their private quarters by ascending the black walnut staircase commissioned by Margaret Beekman Livingston. We know that the staircase was the last element of the house to be rebuilt after the house was burned by the British because Mrs. Livingston lamented in a letter that the "stair" had not yet been completed due to "want of plank" when Martha Washington visited in 1782. The black walnut used to build the stairway came from the property, as did the wood used to replace the original treads in the 1880s.

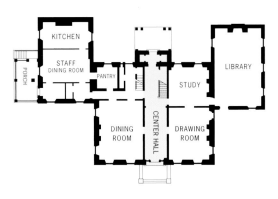

A separate set of servants' stairs connects with the main stairway at the landing. A woodbox was constructed over the hall next to the servants' stairs so that they could replenish fuel in the fireplaces located in the family bedrooms.

Above the landing is a wood and gilt eagle that originally was housed in the American embassy in Paris at the time Chancellor Livingston was Minister to France. The Chancellor brought it back to America and displayed it over his bed until his death.

At the top of the stairs is a swinging gate made of black walnut to blend in with the eighteenth century stairway. Alice Livingston had the gate installed in the early twentieth century to keep children and dogs at bay when the adults were entertaining below.

Drawing Room

The front parlor, called the drawing room by the Livingston family, was traditionally located to the right side of the center hall in a Georgian house. It was here that George Washington, Alexander Hamilton, the Marquis de Lafayette and other distinguished guests would have been welcomed by Margaret Beekman Livingston in the 1700s. In the twentieth century Alice Delafield Clarkson Livingston took tea with her guests in this room after they had signed the guest book.

Clermont's drawing room was the site of Janet Livingston's nuptials to General Richard Montgomery, the tragic "Hero of Quebec," in 1773, and the wedding of her youngest sister Alida to General John Armstrong in 1789. Family tradition also holds that Margaret Beekman Livingston would greet her slaves on Christmas morning

John Henry Livingston's guest book bears the signatures of distinguished visitors to Clermont in the early twentieth century.

Christina Ten Broeck, wife of Philip Livingston (the Signer), gazes out at contemporary visitors from above the Broadwood and Sons square piano.

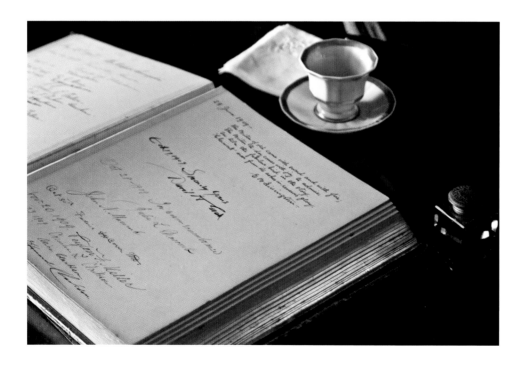

in this room to distribute gold coins and handkerchiefs as presents. The drawing room was the site of somber occasions as well. During the nineteenth century deceased members of the family would be laid out in this room for their loved ones to pay their respects before burial in the family vault on the grounds at Clermont or at nearby St. Paul's Church.

The room is furnished with objects associated with all seven generations of the family. Family portraits displayed here include Abraham Delanoy's depiction of Philip Livingston, signer of the Declaration of Independence, and Gerardus Duykinck's rendering of a young Henry Beekman, brother of Margaret Beekman Livingston. Henry died at the age of 21, leaving his sister the sole heir to an immense estate in Dutchess and Ulster Counties.

This nineteenth century vermeil tea service enhanced the décor of Alice Livingston's dining room but was rarely, if ever, used.

Perhaps the most important object displayed in the drawing room is a gilded French mantel clock based on a model of a never completed monument by Houdon. The monument was slated to be built in the Place de la Concorde before the French Revolution erupted; the guillotine was erected on the site instead. The clock commemorates the balloon flight of aeronauts Jacques Charles and Nicholas Robert on December 1, 1783. This first manned hydrogen gas balloon flight was witnessed by Benjamin Franklin and John Jay, who vividly described the event in a letter to his friend, Chancellor Robert Livingston. The clock is one of two known to exist. Its mate is housed in the Air and Space Museum in Paris.

Robert R. Livingston's French balloon clock (left) embodies the Chancellor's lifelong interest in improving land, sea and air transportation.

The Study

Upon entering this room the visitor's eye is immediately drawn to the mounted head of a moose over the doorway leading to the south wing. The moose-head was a gift to John Henry Livingston from a kinsman whose passions included hunting and taxidermy. Honoria and Janet Livingston took delight as children in racing into the study, leaping, and stretching out to touch the moose's nose. Honoria McVitty recalled as an older woman that when she finally was able to touch the moose on his nose without jumping she knew she was on the verge of adulthood.

The back parlor, now known as the study, has seen many uses over the past three centuries. Once Margaret Beekman Livingston became too infirm to climb the stairs to the second floor she made the small parlor her bedroom. Margaret's son-in-law, Edward Philip Livingston,

The draped woman and dog sculpted by Alice Livingston (below) is one of nearly thirty works by the artist in Clermont's collections. The terracotta bas relief sculpture in the fireplace mantel (right) depicts Honoria and Janet Livingston with their dogs and governess.

made this room his library and was responsible for building the bookcases. Many of the family's prized books, including a set of Diderot's famous *Encyclopedia,* are still housed here.

The room is set up today as Alice Livingston's study and sewing room. The papier maché and mother-of-pearl inlay sewing table was a wedding gift to Clermont and Cornelia Livingston in 1844. Mrs. Livingston's writing desk also was originally owned by Clermont Livingston. Over the fireplace mantel is a gilt mirror attributed to Charles-Honoré Lannuier that originally hung in the saloon of the early Fulton–Livingston steamboat "Chancellor Livingston."

Alice Livingston's sculptured figurines adorn the bookshelves. A bas-relief entablature in the fireplace mantel depicts Mrs. Livingston's young daughters, Honoria and Janet, frolicking in the garden with their (much idealized) governess and dogs, Gobi and Peggy. Mrs. Livingston took up sculpting to entertain her children while they were recovering from the measles in Italy, but she displayed such talent that she later exhibited her work at galleries in Paris and Philadelphia.

The Library

Edward P. Livingston built the south wing in 1831 (originally only 1½ stories) both to balance the house and because he needed additional bedroom space for his growing family. Although a single great room now occupies the entire first floor of this wing, it originally accommodated two bedrooms and a nursery.

The present oak-paneled room was constructed for John Henry Livingston in the 1890s following the death of his second wife, Emily Evans. It initially served as a billiards room and gentleman's retreat. Mark Popkin's portrait of Mr. Livingston still oversees the racks for cues and balls.

John Henry Livingston's portrait (below) hangs above his billiard ball rack. His grandfather, Edward Philip Livingston (right), served as Lieutenant Governor of New York State.

The third Mrs. John Henry Livingston (Alice Delafield Clarkson) had the pool table removed following the arrival of the couple's two daughters. She redecorated the room as the de-facto living room or family room. Works of art and furnishings from the Livingstons' travels—including an early eighteenth century Italian burl walnut desk, an Egyptian bench and mirrors depicting the Four Seasons—were imported to soften what had been a decidedly masculine room.

At one time this room housed a piano and music stand for Honoria and Janet Livingston. Honoria played piano, while Janet accompanied her on her violin. The Livingston girls also enjoyed playing records of Italian opera performances in this room as they read from the family's impressive collection of books.

As in most of the formal rooms of the house, a selection of family portraits is on display. Edward Philip Livingston and Clermont Livingston were the fourth and fifth generation masters of the house. General Matthew Clarkson, who saw action at Saratoga and who was present at Cornwallis' surrender at Yorktown, was an ancestor of Alice Livingston.

Swiss and Italian landscape paintings exhibited at either end of the room over the fireplace mantel and desk were executed by Montgomery Livingston. A bon vivant and something of a rebel, Livingston also painted many American landscapes and is recognized as a minor member of the Hudson River School of art.

The blue paint on the walls above the oak paneling and bookcases is not original. Alice Livingston had the room "painted blue for a change" in 1946, covering a gold embossed wallpaper.

A young French duchess, portrayed in a mezzotint the Livingstons brought back from Italy, stands watch over crystal decanters; the gilded charioteer races past a landscape by John Laporte, c. 1830.

Dining Room

*Thomas Sully's portrait of Andrew Jackson,
the Hero of New Orleans, has watched
over family meals in Clermont's dining
room since the 1860s.*

The encased model of Arryl House was made by Richmond Clarkson from natural materials growing on the grounds at Clermont shortly after the house burned in 1909.

The family dining room has been the first room to the left of the west entry since the first Georgian mansion was built circa 1740. The dining room, like the drawing room, is associated with both joyous gatherings and times of sadness and loss. Margaret Beekman Livingston was celebrated around the colonies for her hospitality. It seems appropriate then that she died of a stroke during lunch, seated with family and friends, at her dining room table.

The dining room table was also where an exhausted John Henry Livingston, his face and hands caked with soot, sat on a windy evening in November 1909 to write about his sense of loss as Chancellor Livingston's 1792 mansion (known as Arryl House or Idele) burned to the ground. Mr. Livingston later asserted that an ember from a

New York Central Railroad locomotive started the fire. Evidence in his letter, however, indicates that a leaf pile being burned on the lawn nearby had gotten out of control and ignited the grass fire that swept over the neoclassical mansion. A rustic model of Arryl House displayed in the dining room, made by a cousin of Mr. Livingston, recalls that event.

The dining room is now painted a pale yellow, as described by architectural historian Van Cortlandt Hubbard during a visit to Clermont in the 1930s. An oddity in this room is the single electrical outlet, installed for a small lamp to aid the butler. John Henry Livingston, a Victorian gentleman to the core, preferred to dine by candlelight. His widow continued the tradition. The warm glow from paired English silver candelabra made for Chancellor Robert Livingston illuminated dinner parties at Clermont until 1962.

John Wollaston's circa 1750 portrait of Margaret Beekman Livingston captures some of the steely determination that led her to rebuild her family's home during the Revolutionary War after British soldiers burned it in 1777.

MARGARET BEEKMAN.
Wife of Justice Robert R. Livingston.

Among the cherished family possessions are a pair of pier tables attributed to Charles-Honoré Lannuier, several saber-leg dining room chairs attributed to the workshop of Duncan Phyfe and Chancellor Livingston's porcelain ice cream urn, made for him in Paris by the firm of Darte-Frères. The pier mirror between the twin doors on the east wall is said to have been carted away by Margaret Beekman Livingston moments before the arrival of British soldiers in 1777.

John Wollaston's portraits of a young Margaret Beekman Livingston and her husband, Judge Robert Livingston, flank the door to the center hall. Portraits of Alice Livingston and her daughters Honoria and Janet grace the corners of the room. The most notable portrait displayed in room is not of a Livingston at all, but of Andrew Jackson; Thomas Sully's portrait of the *Hero of New Orleans* was widely reproduced on handbills during Jackson's successful campaign for the Presidency. How did it come to be here? No one really knows. President Jackson did name Edward Livingston, Chancellor Livingston's youngest brother, Secretary of State and Ambassador to France.

The Kitchen and Pantry

The room seen by visitors today was the third kitchen at Clermont. The original eighteenth century kitchen was located in the basement directly underneath the dining room. When the north wing was constructed in 1814 a large new kitchen was built on the ground floor. During the last major remodeling of the mansion in 1893 the kitchen was relocated to the upper floor, while the basement was converted to use as the laundry room.

When the north wing was first built the upper floor served as Edward P. Livingston's office. This is where tenant farmers came to pay their annual rent and to discuss how they would fulfill their obligation to provide "three days' riding," or labor. After Clermont Livingston inherited the estate his son, John Henry Livingston, made this room his bedroom.

The kitchen is now painted in a maroon and gray scheme that dates to the 1920s. The kitchen is equipped with a coal-burning cast iron stove and hot water heater similar to those used in the early twentieth century. There was also an oak ice box in the room, which used ice drawn from ponds at Clermont. The floor covering was a black and white checkered linoleum.

At the time of John Henry Livingston's death a large table was situated beneath the skylight near the center of the room, where the domestic staff dined on odds and ends of fine china handed down by the Livingston family.

The pass-through leads to the pantry where some staples were kept and flatware and tableware was stored. Final food preparation was also undertaken in this room by the butler. John Henry Livingston owned nearly a dozen sets of porcelain that he and his ancestors had acquired from America, Europe and China between 1780 and 1927. Depending upon the season, a visitor to Clermont today may find the dining room table set with John Henry Livingston's Meissen tableware, Chancellor Livingston's Darte-Frères service or eighteenth century Chinese export porcelain.

Upstairs Hall

The second floor hall once led to four bedrooms, mirroring the original layout of the first floor of the mansion. One of those bedrooms was later converted into a hall which leads to the south wing, as well as a breakfast room and a bathroom.

At the west end of the hall is a small sewing room, added in the 1890s. This room, with its superb view of the river and Catskills, was used by both the family and the domestic staff.

The ceiling in the hall differs from that found elsewhere in the house. It is made of a material called lincrusta. Similar in composition to linoleum, it could be fashioned to resemble leather or other malleable materials. This early example of lincrusta has been crafted to resemble a simple tin ceiling.

The sliding pocket door on the north side of the hallway leads to servants' bedrooms created when the mansion was enlarged in 1874. On the table next to the pocket door is a single candlestick, which was used to light the way to the family bedrooms when thunderstorms knocked out electrical power, something that happened with alarming frequency when Honoria and Janet Livingston were children.

Alice Livingston's Bedroom

Alice Delafield Clarkson Livingston moved into this bedroom following the death of her husband, John Henry Livingston, in 1927. John Henry and Alice Livingston had previously retired to the master bedroom suite that occupied the second and third floors of the South Wing of the mansion. This part of the house, which included his and her bedrooms and bathrooms, a dressing room and a nursery, now houses storage rooms for the study collections.

Mrs. Livingston chose this room because she enjoyed the morning light and because the room looked out on the walled garden and landscape she had designed to the northeast of the house. Gardening was Mrs. Livingston's chief joy in life aside from her family. Even after she had moved out of the mansion and into a cottage on the estate in 1942 she continued to tend her gardens well into her eighties.

One peculiarity of this room is the wardrobe, which was built into the corner of the room to conceal a raised portion of the floor that provided headroom to domestic staff using the servants' stairs. A tall person ascending the stairs actually has his head accommodated by space in the bottom of the wardrobe in the adjoining room!

The Blue Guest Bedroom

This room belonged to Honoria Livingston when she was a child. She and her sister moved into the south wing bedrooms after their father's death.

This room was the prized guest bedroom, in part because of its river view. The window next to the fireplace looks out on Clermont's dock, the official port-of-registry of the first steamboat. Next to the window is a French dressing table, said to have been a wedding gift to Robert Fulton and Harriet Livingston from Chancellor Robert R. Livingston.

The twin beds were originally a single rope bed. The head boards decorated with a pineapple finial were the headboard and footboard to the original bed. The reason why the Livingstons chose to make two beds from one is a mystery, but perhaps it is related to their frugal Scottish heritage. Recycling—of furnishings, architectural elements and organic waste—was a tradition at Clermont long before the contemporary environmental movement.

The room appears today as it was furnished when Reginald "Rex" McVitty was courting Honoria Livingston during the summer of 1930.

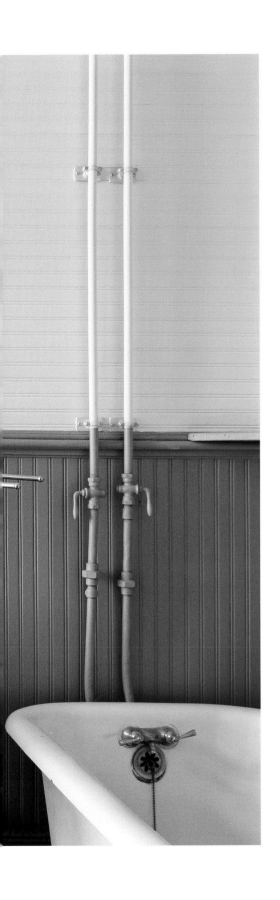

Bathrooms

The bathroom off the guest bedroom is one of nine full baths and two water closets in the house. Indoor plumbing was installed in the 1890s and is said to have been designed by John Henry Livingston, who fancied himself a clever amateur plumber—perhaps too clever. The convoluted plumbing baffled the men whom Alice Livingston brought in to revive the water supply system in an aborted effort to reopen the mansion as a year-round residence after the Second World War.

Water was brought to the house by gravity from a buried concrete cistern on the hill overlooking the carriage barn. As it entered the house the water was directed to one of two metal cisterns located in the attic. Gravity then fed the water through a series of interior pipes.

A window above the bathtub often perplexes visitors. It was installed to provide lighting in a closet located off the center hall behind the bathroom in the days before the mansion was wired for electricity.

All of the family and guest bedrooms were provided with a private bath or water closet. Three bathrooms were shared by the servants who occupied the five bedrooms on the third floor.

Servants' Rooms

The African-American slaves who tended to the domestic needs of the Livingston family in the eighteenth century had bedrooms in the basement or lived in cottages south of the mansion, between the house and the dock. The basement bedrooms were finished and were comfortably cool in the summer. Martha Washington is said to have stayed in one of these basement rooms during a week-long visit in June 1782.

In 1874 the roof of the mansion was raised above the original Georgian block and the domestic staff was moved into bedrooms in the garret. According to the 1875 New York State census five domestic servants lived in the house at that time. Slavery had been abolished in New York in 1821 and the enslaved African-American domestic staff had been replaced with newly arrived immigrants from Ireland, England and Germany, as well as American girls of Palatine descent from nearby farms.

Janet Livingston took immediately to the wheel, while her sister Honoria sat demurely in the back seat when the Livingston family's first motorcar arrived at Clermont in 1919.

Clermont's domestic staff reached its peak just before World War I. The staff in 1915 included a coachman, head gardener, two assistant gardeners, a lady's maid, a nursery girl, a kitchen maid, a laundress, a chamber maid, a cook and a waitress. Staff members hailed from Switzerland, Finland, Denmark, Norway, Ireland and Germany.

Olivek Christrian, the Danish nursery girl and governess, later stirred up "great excitement" on the estate according to Honoria McVitty when she married coachman Christopher Myers. The Myerses eventually moved to the Bronx, but "Nurse Oli" kept in touch with her former charges until they were well past middle age.

By the time of the Wall Street Crash of 1929 the domestic staff had been reduced to three resident workers, all African-American natives of South Carolina. Clarence Jones was Clermont's butler, while his wife Louise handled the cook's duties. They were assisted by laundress Laura Pugh.

Janet (left) and Honoria Livingston (right) pose with "Nurse Oli" and their favorite dolls upstairs at Clermont in 1913.

Festivities

Chronology

The Owners of Clermont, 1728–1962

Title to the house at Clermont passed, by custom, from father to eldest son until the death of Chancellor Robert R. Livingston in 1813. The Chancellor's will broke precedent by granting title to his eldest daughter, Elizabeth, rather than to her husband (and third cousin), Edward P. Livingston.

1728–1775
Robert Livingston, Jr., the Builder (1688–1775)

1775–1775
Robert R. Livingston, the Judge (1718–1775)

1775–1813
Robert R. Livingston, Jr., the Chancellor (1746–1813)

1813–1829
Elizabeth Stevens Livingston (1780–1829)

1829–1843
Edward Philip Livingston (1779–1843)

1843–1895
Clermont Livingston (1817–1895)

1895–1896
Katharine Livingston (later Timpson) (1873–1933)

1896–1927
John Henry Livingston (1848–1927)

1927–1962
Alice Delafield Clarkson Livingston (1872–1964)

Heads-of-Household at Clermont, 1728–1962

The head-of-household at Clermont, as determined by census records and practical considerations, was not always the person who held legal title to the property. Most notably, Margaret Beekman Livingston never owned the mansion, but she held a life tenancy from her son and it was commonly considered "Madame Livingston's house."

1728–1775
Robert Livingston, Jr., the Builder (1688–1775)

1775–1775
Robert R. Livingston, the Judge (1718–1775)

1775–1800
Margaret Beekman Livingston (1724–1800)

1800–1843
Edward Philip Livingston (1779–1843)

1843–1869
Clermont Livingston (1817–1895)

1869–1874
Frederick Watts DePeyster (1842–1874)

1874–1876
Mary Livingston DePeyster (1845–1876)

1876–1927
John Henry Livingston (1848–1927)

1927–1962
Alice Delafield Clarkson Livingston (1872–1964)

Timeline

1600s

1683
Siege of Vienna marks the high tide of the Ottoman Empire's advance into Europe

1666
Great Fire of London

1661
Charles II crowned King of England and Louis XIV begins to build Versailles

1689
William of Orange and his wife, Mary, become King and Queen of England, crowned after accepting the Declaration of Rights, in which royal prerogatives are diminished and the people, through Parliament, are granted civil and political rights

1700s

1701–1714
War of the Spanish Succession

1732
Benjamin Franklin publishes Poor Richard's Almanack

1740
Frederick the Great crowned King of Prussia

1746
Britain defeats Scots under Stuart Pretender "Bonny Prince Charles" at Culloden Moor

Around the World

1675   **1700**   **1725**

The Livingstons

December 13, 1654
Robert Livingston is born to Rev. John Livingston and Janet Fleming in Ancram, Scotland

June 1673
Robert Livingston arrives in Charlestown, Massachusetts aboard the *Catharine*

July 22, 1686
Robert Livingston receives a patent for the Manor of Livingston from English Governor Thomas Dongan

July 24, 1688
Robert Livingston, Jr., third son of Robert Livingston and Alida Schuyler, is born at Albany

November 1699
Robert Livingston, Jr. arrives in Glasgow to be educated under the direction of his Scottish uncles

October 1, 1728
Robert Livingston, Jr. inherits 13,000 acres, later known as the Clermont estate, under his father's will

November 27, 1746
Robert R. Livingston, Jr., later known as Chancellor Livingston, is born in New York City

Circa 1745
Robert Livingston, Jr. builds a Georgian manor house on his Clermont estate, incorporating part of an earlier brick and stone house

December 8, 1742
Robert R. Livingston, son of Robert Livingston, Jr., marries Margaret Beekman

1751
iderot begins
ublishing his famous
ncyclopedie

1756–1763
Seven Years War, known
as the French and Indian
War in America

1765
James Watt invents the
steam engine

1773
Boston Tea Party

1776
Adam Smith publishes
The Wealth of Nations

1775
The American Revolution
begins with the Battle of
Lexington and Concord

1778
Captain James Cook
"discovers" Hawaii

1787
Constitution of the
United States signed

1789
French Revolution
begins with the storming
of the Bastille

1799
George Washington dies
at Mount Vernon

1793
Louis XVI and Marie
Antoinette executed

1804
Napoleon Bonaparte
proclaims himself
Emperor of France

Early 1800s

1812
Napoleon invades Russia
and the United States
declares war on Great
Britain

1815
Napoleon defeated by
Wellington at Waterloo
and is banished to
St. Helena

1824
Mexico becomes a
republic and Simon
Bolivar liberates Peru

1846–1848
Mexican War

1833
Parliament
abolishes slavery in
the British Empire

1837
Victoria crowned Queen
of Great Britain, which
she will rule until 1901

1848
Karl Marx and Friedrich
Engels publish *The
Communist Manifesto*

1775   **1800**   **1825**

October 1765
Judge Robert R.
Livingston appointed as
delegate to the Stamp
Act Congress

October 1777
British troops under
the command of
General John Vaughan
burn the manor house
at Clermont

June 11, 1776
Robert R. Livingston, Jr.
elected to the
Committee of Five,
charged by the
Continental Congress to
draft a Declaration of
Independence

December 1775
Judge Robert R.
Livingston dies of a
stroke six months after
the death of his father,
Robert of Clermont

April 30, 1789
Chancellor Livingston
gives the oath of office
to George Washington
as first President of the
United States

September 17, 1792
Chancellor Livingston
writes to Samuel Mitchill
that he has spent the
year building a new
house, known later as
Arryl House

June 1800
Margaret Beekman
Livingston dies
at Clermont

May 2, 1803
The Louisiana Purchase,
negotiated by Chancellor
Livingston, is signed
by the Chancellor,
James Monroe, and the
French Finance Minister

August 17, 1807
The maiden voyage
of Robert Livingston's
and Robert Fulton's
"steam-boat" made
between New York City
and Clermont

February 26, 1813
Chancellor Robert R.
Livingston dies at Clermont
and is interred in the
family vault on the estate

November 3, 1843
Edward P. Livingston dies
at "Old Clermont," ten
months after the death
of his brother-in-law,
Robert L. Livingston,
owner of the Chancellor's
neoclassical house

September 15, 1824
The Marquis de Lafayette visits
Clermont and attends a
banquet at the home of Robert L.
and Margaret Maria Livingston

1830 to 1832
Edward Philip Livingston
serves as Lt. Governor
of New York State

July 8, 1848
John Henry Livingston is
born to Clermont and
Cornelia Livingston at
"Oak Hill" near Hudson,
New York

Late 1800s

1861–1865
American Civil War

1879
Thomas Edison invents
practical electric light

1876
Alexander Bell patents
the telephone

1869
First transcontinental
railroad completed in
the United States

1870–1871
Franco-Prussian War

1900s

1914
World War One begins
after the assassination
of Austrian Archduke
Franz Ferdinand

1903
The first powered,
heavier-than-air plane is
flown at Kitty Hawk by
Wilbur and Orville Wright

1927
Charles Lindbergh
makes first solo trans-
Atlantic flight

1896
First modern Olympic
games are held in
Athens, Greece

1909
The NAACP is founded
in New York, led by
W.E.B. DuBois

1929
The Stock Market Crash
in October sets off
the Great Depression,
lasting through 1938

1905
Albert Einstein develops
his theory of relativity

1939
The Second World War
begins when Hitler's
Germany invades Poland

1898
Spanish-American War;
Theodore Roosevelt elected
Governor of New York

1919
Prohibition enacted in
the United States

1875

1900

1925

August 1855
Hudson River School
artist Montgomery
Livingston dies and his
house is sold to Emily
and Anna Clarkson

November 9, 1906
John Henry Livingston
marries Alice Delafield
Clarkson and departs
for a two-year trip to
Europe and Africa

January 27, 1927
John Henry Livingston
dies at the family's
winter home, "The
Bandbox," in Aiken,
South Carolina

January 9, 1872
Alice Delafield Clarkson
is born to Howard and
Alice Clarkson

November 4, 1895
Clermont Livingston, grandson of Chancellor Livingston,
dies at Arryl House

November 1917
Honoria and Janet Livingston
visit Washington, D.C. at the
beginning of a visit to the South
"for the duration" of World War I

November 1898
John Henry Livingston,
running for Congress as
a Democrat in a heavily
Republican district,
is defeated by a handful
of votes

November 2, 1871
John Henry Livingston
marries Catherine
Hamersley, who died
two years later after
giving birth to their only
child, Katharine

September 12, 1931
Honoria Alice Livingston
marries Reginald McVitty at
St. Paul's Church in Tivoli

February 7, 1909
Honoria Alice Livingston
is born to John Henry
and Alice Livingston,
followed a year later by
the birth of Janet
Cornelia Livingston

May 1942
Alice Livingston moves
out of the manor house
and into Clermont
Cottage also called the
Gardener's Cottage

1964
Congress adopts the Gulf
of Tonkin Resolution
beginning a major escala-
tion of the Vietnam War

November 4, 2008
Barack Obama elected
President of the United
States of America

1946–1989
The Cold War

2000s

1969
Apollo 11's Neil
Armstrong becomes the
first human to set foot
on the Moon

1989
The Berlin Wall is
breached, leading to
the fall of the
Communist Bloc

1962
The Cuban Missile Crisis
brings the world to the
brink of nuclear war

1979
The Shah of Iran is over-
thrown and is replaced
by Islamist leader
Ayatollah Khomeini

Around the World

1975   2000   2010

The Livingstons

June 2, 1962
The State of New York
acquires the mansion
and nearly 400 acres of
the Clermont estate
from Alice Livingston
for $175,000

July 30, 1979
Reginald "Rex" McVitty
dies at Sylvan Cottage
at Clermont

June 21, 2000
Honoria Livingston McVitty
dies at the age of 91 in
Sarasota, Florida

April 20, 1964
Alice Delafield Clarkson
Livingston dies at
Clermont Cottage

July 1986
More than 300 descen-
dants of the first Robert
Livingston gather at
Clermont to celebrate
the 300th anniversary
of the founding of
Livingston Manor

August 15, 1972
Janet Cornelia
Livingston dies at
Roosevelt Hospital in
New York City

1977
The Friends of Clermont
chartered by the New
York State Department
of Education

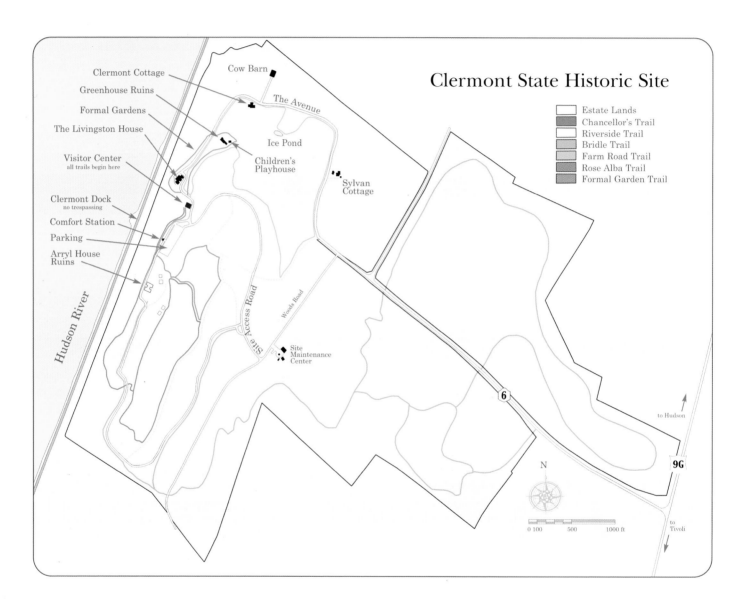

Clermont Cottage
Greenhouse Ruins
Formal Gardens
The Livingston House

Cow Barn
The Avenue
Ice Pond
Children's Playhouse

Sylvan Cottage

Visitor Center
all trails begin here

Clermont Dock
no trespassing

Comfort Station

Parking

Arryl House
Ruins

Hudson River

Site Access Road

Woods Road

Site Maintenance Center

Clermont State Historic Site

	Estate Lands
	Chancellor's Trail
	Riverside Trail
	Bridle Trail
	Farm Road Trail
	Rose Alba Trail
	Formal Garden Trail

6

9G

to Hudson

to Tivoli

N

0 100   500   1000 ft

Photographic credits: Chris Kendall: pages 38–80, 88–89, 96, and back cover;
Tracie Rozhon: cover and pages 6–7, 23–37, 84–87;
Historic photographs on pages 9, 11, 15, 17, 19–22, and 82–83 are courtesy of Clermont State Historic Site,
New York State Office of Parks, Recreation and Historic Preservation; portrait of Robert Fulton on page 19
is courtesy of Fenimore Art Museum, Cooperstown, New York (photograph by Richard Walker)

Special thanks go to Eliot Hawkins and J. Winthrop Aldrich, who assiduously helped with the editing
of this book; to Anne Cassidy, who gathered the historic photographs for the book; and to Joan K. Davidson
and Ann Birckmayer at Furthermore: a program of the J. M. Kaplan Fund.

Finally, warm thanks to the board, staff, and membership of the Friends of Clermont—
the organization that has long wanted to see such a book in the hands of visitors to this magnificent site
and has been instrumental in making it happen.